Testimonials

"Master Sean is an amazing coach, but to me he's more than that, he is my big brother. He had the ability to teach me the vision to give me the motivation and courage to make me a champion."
– Daba Modibo Keita,
2-time World Champion, 2-time Olympian

From students and parents:

"His students learn the value of working hard, the importance of setting goals, and how to persevere until they make themselves proud!"

"Mr. Ramey has been helping my child with focusing on goals. He is the best! I cannot say enough positive things about his program."

"Sometimes in life, you are lucky enough to meet someone who changes your life or the life of others. Someone who really makes a difference. Someone who pushes you to your limits and helps you reach your goals. Someone who lets you know you can achieve your dream and helps you reach it. I knew the first time I met Sean Ramey, that he was that kind of person."

"Master Ramey's dedication to his students and the community has proven him to be an advocate for family values. His commitment to teaching moral excellence, diligent work ethic, and persevering attitudes produce better citizens and stronger families."

"Under the guidance of Mr. Ramey, I have gained the confidence in dealing with my day-to-day endeavors."

"I am a different person after participating in Sean Ramey's program. I think differently, I don't overreact to things that usually upset me in the past, I view myself differently than I once did. I now know that I can achieve the goals I set for myself."

"Sean is a master of instilling personal confidence, pride, drive and excellence!"

"His program endorses hard work and builds character. My daughter has gained confidence and self-esteem. We are thankful for this."

Creating the Champion Within

Sean Ramey

A Champs in Life Publication

Copyright

ISBN 979-8-9899465-0-1

Written by Sean Ramey

Published by Amber Light Publishing
www.AmberLightPublishing.com

Editing and Book Design by Nita Robinson
Nita Helping Hand? www.NitaHelpingHand.com

Cover Design by www.KAM.design

Illustrations by Kinsley Ramey

Contents

Dedication

To my amazing family, thank you for all your Love, Support, and Patience.

To my daughter, Kinsley Ramey, thank you for the amazing illustrations.

Thank you, Nita Robinson-Lewis, for your guidance in bringing this to light.

To all the Champions in life, thank you. Without your journeys, this wouldn't have been possible.

Introduction

It is amazing how many billions are spent on the building or shaping of our bodies, our careers, and our education, but the focus and importance of building and shaping how we think is neglected.

How we act, what we do, and what we achieve all starts with the mind. How we think, how we view ourselves, and how we handle failure, decide if and when we achieve our goals. I hope you are able to learn and take away a few things from this easy and fast read. And best of success in Creating Your Champion Within!

Failure

Fail Often and Fail Fast

Failure should not be such a bad word. However, it is not necessarily our fault for thinking it is. We were all raised at a young age knowing that an "F" in school is the worst grade you can get. We all knew what it stood for – **FAIL.** When actually Failure **can** be a better teacher than success. When we succeed, we tend to ignore what we can improve upon. Failure allows us to get back to the drawing board and find out how we can fix whatever did not work. When you win all the time, you quit believing you have anything to learn or improve upon.

Some of the best lessons are those that were learned the hardest or hurt the most. That means losing, not getting chosen for the team, not achieving that A in our class, or getting passed over for that promotion. I would wager a large sum of money that when Michael Jordan was not selected for his High School Varsity team, that played a huge part in him becoming, arguably, the greatest basketball player in history.

"The key to Success is Failure." – Michael Jordan

Fail forward, not backward. Failing forward means you learned something by failing that put you in a better position than you were originally. Maybe you found something you can improve upon; maybe that loss started a fire and introduced you to a new level of intensity and motivation. Failing backward means that you learned nothing, and blamed everything and everybody on the loss except yourself. You also plan on improving upon nothing, because you think it was a fluke and it probably won't happen again.

If one has not accumulated a list of failures, one has not challenged themselves enough. It is important to continually challenge yourself in order to reach new heights. And when you continually challenge yourself, there will be times you Fail, Lose, or not end up on top of the podium. You have to learn to accept that. Failure must come before big wins and big achievements. Think of Failure as a small practice test before the big final. This will allow you to brush up on certain skills or knowledge that will ensure you win the big game. So, in fact, you should welcome failure... then LEARN from it.

Our own self-doubts and fear are the single biggest dream crushers of happiness that we have. And it lives in us daily. It is your choice whether you decide to listen to it or not.

"Fail often, fail your way to success."
– Thomas Edison on inventing the light bulb

Failure is not what has destroyed most dreams, it is the **Fear of Failing** that has. Just the thought of failing alone paralyzes most people into never trying something outside of their comfort zone.

It is unfortunate that most people do not realize that failure usually comes before success. So fail now, fail first, and fail often! Get it out of the way so success can follow!

Start believing and understanding that failure is a part of the process. When you accept that, you do not fear it, you deal with it and then learn from it.

The toughest times lie just before your biggest breakthroughs. When you feel like quitting the most, that is usually the point just before your breakthrough is about to happen. It has been said that 97% of all fears never happen. So, stop being afraid and paralyzed by "what-ifs". Many times, failure weeds out those who are not serious about succeeding.

It is the thought of failure that keeps people from taking action. Whatever you fear and do not face, will forever own you. When you face that fear, you begin to learn how to deal with it, then eliminate it.

Playing the victim does nothing to help you succeed or grow. And sometimes good things fall apart so better things can fall together. This is why people or businesses become complacent... Hardships and failures allow better things and experiences to happen. As long as things are "Good" no one is willing to change to become "Great". When a person is comfortable being "Good", that will lead to average. Average people will always follow the masses. It is more comfortable to do that. More often than not, the ones who stand out and achieve massive success are the ones who went in the opposite direction of the masses. Going in the opposite direction is definitely not a safe play. However, you cannot achieve your Goals by playing it safe. It takes preparation, it takes a plan, it takes courage, and it takes action.

I have noticed the difference between those that are Good and those that are Great is where those individuals place "blame". Good sometimes blame others; the Greats take responsibility and all the blame.

On Being Average

I expect my daughter to be a success in whatever she chooses. It is her duty to us and especially to herself. She was and is given every opportunity to succeed. So, success is the only option. Success is her duty.

I say that only because so many have done amazing, groundbreaking things with so much less. Also, it is important to have high standards, not just for yourself, but for your children. It is a fact that when you expect more, they achieve more. Just like yourself; when you expect more of yourself, you do more.

Average is dangerous because it is acceptable; therefore, we get comfortable with it. Average never did anything great.

"Good is the enemy of Great." – *Tony Robbins*

Being average means you are setting yourself up for a lifetime of misery, hard times, and countless years of unfulfilled dreams and wishes.

Remember, it is crowded at the bottom. You are bound to get lost in the mix.

Routines are good, but to get to different heights and levels, you must do difficult things, things that sometimes make you uncomfortable.

Greatness lies outside your comfort zone.

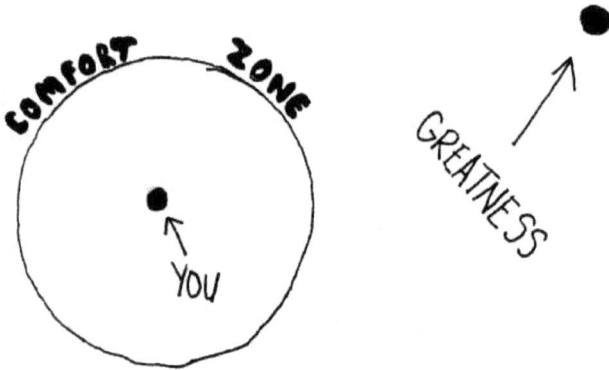

Growth begins when times are uncomfortable. Get comfortable being uncomfortable. Comfortable = Complacency. Complacency is the enemy to greatness.

"The cave you fear holds the treasure you seek."
– J.P. Sears

Always be upgrading the current version of yourself; your phones and tablets do it, so why shouldn't you?

Some say becoming successful is tough. Try existing in day-to-day life, paycheck to paycheck, bill to bill, and see how hard life is when you are not successful and when you settle for what is easy and average.

To be successful means you have to set numerous goals and expectations for yourself. Goals are dreams with deadlines. Dreams without deadlines are just that... Dreams. It is easy to talk about what your dreams are, but have you come up with a plan to make them a reality? Have you set a date by which you plan to achieve that dream? The masses are masters at stating what their dreams are but fail miserably when it comes to executing a plan in order to achieve those dreams. So, before you think about or should we say "dream" about that next accomplishment, do these three crucial things:

1. Write down your Goals and place them somewhere you see them every day (bathroom mirror, refrigerator, desk, etc.).
2. Design a plan that will allow you to achieve that Goal. This plan may change as time progresses.
3. Put down a date that you plan on achieving that Goal. This is extremely important! All goals and dreams *need* deadlines!

Do all 3 of these steps. Do not skip one. Many just think about their Goals, but you must literally write it down so you see it, every waking day. You must <u>see</u> it in order to **believe** it, and when you begin to believe it, you will **achieve** it.

See, Believe, Achieve

Remember that what got you to where you currently are probably will not get you to where you want to be. This is why you must stop seeking comfort. Growth is uncomfortable, but growth is necessary if you want to continually improve and achieve greater things. I have always been told that if you are not *Growing*, you are *Dying*. Time waits for no one; therefore, if you stay where you were, you have actually regressed.

There needs to be continual growth (physically, mentally, spiritually, emotionally), otherwise, it will be impossible to achieve bigger and better things in your life.

The truth is though, most people are content with "average" because success does not always follow their plans or their timelines. Success, for most, does not happen quick enough or easy enough. That is why many resort back to where they were before, or stay with their current job, or get back with their ex-boyfriend/girlfriend. Sadly, people will always fall back to their comfort zone because it is easy and they feel "comfortable" there. Yet, it is that desire for ease that will make things hard on them later. Goal achieving is not always easy and enjoyable. In fact, anything worth achieving or earning *is not* easy. Your plan may fail once, twice, or several times. It may take a lot longer than expected. It may even be so much more difficult than expected. However, that is what separates the Good from the Great; the Great do not give up on their dreams. The Great put deadlines on their dreams, and formulate a plan to achieve them.

Beware of the Goal Killers: DOUBT, FEAR, and PROCRASTINATION.

Your best friends in achieving Goals are the Dynamic Duo of POSITIVE MINDSET and ACTION.

There is no straight line to success. There will be pitfalls, plateaus, valleys, steep climbs, inclines, mountains, deep water, etc. Those obstacles will be in the form of injuries, low self-esteem, lack of patience, lack of motivation, and even lack of support from friends and family. Yet, if you want to achieve those dreams and goals, you must persevere. There is no quitting.

How you think it will be:

You ————————————————————— goal

How it actually will be:

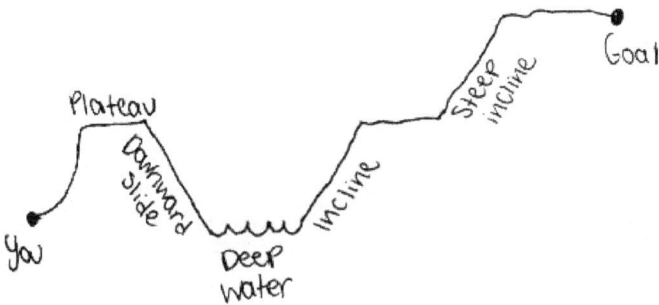

You · Plateau — Downward Slide — Deep water — Incline — Steep incline — Goal

Because things do not go as planned, people give up on their bigger dreams and goals, and become content with average.

The definition of average via Google is "Typical", or "Middle" – and remember, the middle gets squeezed. Ask any working middle class family or individual, how "easy" it is to survive in today's world. Average, while easy to achieve, is difficult to exist. You should seek to become Extraordinary, and to be that is not that hard… just do the "extra" things "ordinary" people do not do. It is truly that simple.

Confidence

Your Modern Day Armor

The best things in life are free… namely confidence.

Confidence cannot be bought in stores; it also does not have an expiration date.

You must believe before you can achieve. Many stresses in life come from the fear of failing. Imagine changing your thinking, of not fearing failure but having the confidence to believe that success follows failure.

Confidence is your armor. It will shield you from jealousy, envy, and the insults that come from them. It is your "thick skin".

Confidence will shield you from insecurities and self-doubt.

Confidence will allow you to keep striving in the face of doubt from others. It will allow your child, or yourself, to stand up against forces like peer pressure.

Our own self-doubt is the single biggest killer to what we do. With no confidence, self-doubt and low self-esteem enter.

Now, it is important to realize that confidence alone is not enough. Confidence has to be backed up with ability. So, do not think you can do everything with confidence, but you can do everything *better* with confidence.

Expect to win only when you have planned and prepared to win. If you skip the planning and preparation, you are displaying what I call *Fake Confidence*. You have confidence only because of the lies you told yourself. That is different than earned confidence that comes from planning and preparation.

One of the most powerful tools in the world is a made-up mind. It makes fortunes, it cures addictions, it wins championships.

Attitude *defines your* ***Altitude*** *in life.* Meaning, your attitude will determine how far you go in this game of life. Confidence is a key in determining your attitude.

Attitude and Gratitude are a championship-winning combination. To be successful you must have a positive, winning attitude. You must also show Gratitude; appreciating where you are at and where you came from. I have always said Gratitude brings Greatness. This removes the thought that anyone owes you anything. Instead, you are grateful for where you are at and who you are. This removes all excuses and blame from your thoughts. Therefore, your belief is, "If it is meant to be, it is up to me." They say it is physiologically impossible to be grateful and angry at the same time. So now, by being grateful, you remove a negative emotion that will hold you back from achieving greatness, such as anger.

The words you speak (and say to yourself) matter! Never give your negativity or pain a **voice**. Never speak it; do not give them the power by stating your fears or pains (void – I am too tired, I can't, I am not good enough, I am not smart enough, etc.). Take these out of your vocabulary.

Many people only pay attention to their weaknesses; this is why they have no confidence. When people start to focus on their strengths, they gain confidence. Focus on your strengths more than your weaknesses.

"You can either master your words and thoughts or they will end up mastering you." – Sean Ramey

What is your X-Factor? What is your "it"? Find it, cultivate it, grow it, maximize it, use it. "It" or X-Factor, is something that makes you stand out, something that makes you different. And yes, we <u>ALL</u> have something that makes us different.

Before you can win the championship game on the floor, you must win the championship game in your mind! How you carry yourself matters, and I am talking about physically. Posture dictates Mindset. Quit slouching and looking at the ground only three feet ahead of you. Get those shoulders back and head up; keep your eyes on the prize in front of you. Before you can be a champ, you have to start acting like one first! When you look weak, people treat you as weak. All of these years teaching martial arts, I have said it countless times; Keep your head high, stand tall, and do not look like an easy target. People see someone who is confident and sure of themselves when they have good posture. This is the first step in being more confident; by carrying yourself as a confident individual.

Confidence is a key driving force in how well you do in whatever it is you want to do. You have to believe in yourself before others will believe in you.

Consider confidence as the fuel to get you to the finish line (your goal). When others give up because it is taking longer than expected or they lose confidence in their abilities, use your confidence in your abilities to power through. That fuel could also be the memory of someone who told you that you could not achieve it or that you were not good enough. Many of the greats resort back to when they were told they could not achieve something, to give them that added push to get across the finish line.

We all know that what we say and think affects how we act. Eliminate, as much as possible, all negative thoughts and words you use to describe yourself (I am stupid, I am ugly, I am not smart enough, I am not qualified, I will never be that good). What you say to yourself, even what you think for the slightest minute, matters.

This will be a gradual process and will take time. All I ask is that you gradually, over time, eliminate those negative thoughts you say to yourself day after day. Remember, master your words and thoughts or they will end up mastering you.

Something that also helps in gaining and maintaining confidence is remembering where you came from. While this may be traumatic for some due to abuse, trauma, or addictions, take time to recognize where you are at. You are alive, breathing, and reading this book. In my eyes, that looks like you are winning. Your past, regardless of how hard it was, could not break you. You defeated every tragedy, accident, abuse, trauma, and sickness you experienced in the past because you are reading this today. Well done, champ. Recognize your growth and appreciate your victories. Victory is yours.

Envy

Jealousy and Envy are Earned

If you find yourself getting upset at people talking behind your back, remember that it is because you are steps **_ahead_** of them. In fact, you should be upset when people are not talking about you. No one envies an average person with average accomplishments. Let it be a sign that when people are talking behind your back, you are making waves. When people stop talking about you, you are not doing anything special or achieving anything worth talking about; you are not making waves… in fact, you are sinking.

"One day, the people that did not believe in you will tell everyone how they met you."
– Johnny Depp

Remember, jealousy and envy are earned. It is a sure sign that you are on the right track and growing. Jealousy comes from people who believe that you are better than them, or that your achievements are greater than theirs. People tend to look down on other's dreams and goals, especially when they believe they cannot achieve it themselves. It is difficult for others to support one's journey when they cannot relate to it themselves.

It is also extremely important to remember that there is no need to envy others' successes. There is enough success to go around. It is an extremely limiting mindset to believe that there is a limited amount of success or achievement. Just because someone achieves or gains some success, it does not take away from your future successes. There will always be enough to go around. When you begin to envy another person's success, it truly limits your possibility of achieving the same or greater.

"New levels create new devils." – T.D. Jakes

Some people cannot be happy or fulfilled until they are unhappy or make others around them unhappy. This may include close friends and family. I am sure you have heard of the saying that *misery loves company.* Well, that is absolutely true. And there will be those that are unhappy until they make those around them unhappy. Sounds crazy, doesn't it? Ever wonder why these gossip magazines and newspapers are so popular? Why is it that reality shows are so popular? People love to watch a trainwreck. People love to watch others fail. People love to see and hear drama. Don't be one of them. Separate yourself as far away as possible from those individuals.

When you raise your status and your place in life, you will always get hate from those who believe they cannot improve upon their life. Usually, the envy comes from those that are doing less or have less than you. Not everyone in your life is going to be happy about your dreams, your successes, or your victories.

Jealousy and envy also make for great fire-starters for your motivation. Ask any top athlete, entrepreneur, CEO, or success story, and they will tell you the naysayers, haters, and people who doubted them, played a crucial role in their success.

Avoid envying others' possessions or place in life. Jealousy and envy truly stunt your growth to the top.

As long as you are focusing on them and what they are doing, you are unable to focus on you and what you are doing. Remember, Winners focus on winning, Losers focus on winners.

Those that continually talk about others and waste time envying others' success, waste their own time and energy in finding their own.

There is no way one can achieve their own success if they are so worried about someone else's success.

Competition

Embrace It

Do not ever shy away from competition. Competition is life. You will compete for anything meaningful in life. Your job, your spouse, your place on a team, your education; your place in life will require you competing for it. Accept it. Embrace it.

It is usually the fear of failing or losing that makes people avoid competition. This can be in school, the workplace, and even in your own family. However, when you compete you tend to try harder at what you are doing. Remember though, that there is "healthy" competition and then there is "unhealthy" competition. Healthy competition raises standards, people are complimented and supported, and it benefits all involved. Whether it is a team, workplace, or a family, people are actually supporting each other to become better and win in what they are competing for. In an unhealthy competition environment, people are wishing for the failure of their fellow competitors, fellow workers, and even fellow family members. Unhealthy competition becomes stressful and toxic, and is actually unenjoyable for everyone involved.

It is ok to be nervous or scared, at times, when you are in a competitive environment. Everyone (even those that you do not believe do) get nervous or have butterflies. The Champions, the ones on the podium, the ones who win or land the position, are the ones who control that fear the best. They are the ones who constantly focus on their goals instead of on their emotions, or on others. Stay focused on *your* goals... Mind *Your* Business!

Since Life itself can be viewed as a competition, it can be also viewed as a game. With that in mind, you cannot sit on the sidelines. Games are meant to be played. You cannot win the game of life if you do not play. Do not watch the game of life; play the game of life. Life is not a spectator sport. It is those that never take a risk or even step on to the playing field that will lose. And you, yourself, will always be your toughest competition. It will be you who talks yourself out of a play, or who talks yourself into stepping on the field and making a play. The field I am referring to is the pathway to your dreams and goals… your sport, your schooling, your career, your family. Those are the playing fields I am talking about. Quitters never win and the scared never start.

The good news is that since life is a game, and while you only have one life, there are several quarters to be played during your life. You will win some of those quarters, and you will lose some of those quarters.

The point is to win more than we lose. If you happen to lose a quarter, suck it up! All the greats have lost…

many more times than us! Your past does not guarantee the outcome of your future.

You can either let your past Define you or Defeat you. Choose one…

Winners find a way to Win, and Losers find a way to Lose.

When you find yourself in a tough fight or close game, remember the three C's.

1. Composure

2. Clarity

3. Commitment

When the pressure starts to build, keep your **composure**. Then keep your **clarity** as to what your ultimate goal is. Finally, stay **committed** to following your game plan for reaching your goal.

Compete with those (even if it is just mentally) that have done what you are wanting to do or be. Be careful competing with only those around you, because they are probably not going to make it to the big leagues (statistically speaking)… and if you constantly compare yourself to and compete with those around you or only on your level, then neither are you. Go Big, Dream Big, Compete Big (even if it is just mentally for the time being).

You will only improve to the level of competition you hold yourself to. Aim High… this includes holding the level of your competition to higher standards. Do not compete with those that have average results or achievements. Chase the top-level earners, the M.V.P's, and those that are where you aspire to be.

Be committed to greatness in everything you do. Work, school, sports, relationships.

Once you meet or surpass that level of competition, you have to elevate your competition. Fight the desire to compete with low level achievers, just because it is an easy win and good for your confidence.

Remember, you are only as good as the level of competition you face. Easy wins breed complacency and average achievements.

When you raise your standard of competition and expectations, it will be uncomfortable at first. This is when growth begins; you begin your ascent to new levels. When the competition begins to get tough and your competitors begin closing in on you, do not fear it, embrace it. You are the knife and the competition is your sharpening stone. Competition makes you sharper, better, and more effective.

Be grateful for your competition. Competition helps you achieve higher levels when you get lazy and complacent. They help you get to levels you normally would not be able to get to by yourself.

Friends

Be Careful Who You Call Friend

Rule #1 – Believe in yourself.

Rule #2 – Surround yourself with people who believe in you because there will be times you stop believing in yourself.

Choose your friends wisely. You are who you surround yourself with. If you hang around trouble, you will get in trouble. If you hang around negative, envious people, you will become negative and envious. It has been said that you are the sum of the five people you hang around most. Therefore, align yourself with those that share your passion, your positivity, and your morals.

First and foremost, your first best friend should be YOURSELF. The person you see when you look in the mirror can be your best friend or your worst enemy. You choose. How can others enjoy your company when you do not even enjoy your company? Remember the first Rule: Believe in Yourself.

Be careful who you call "friend". Are they around you because it benefits them? Do not confuse the fact that people *should* see benefit and value in your friendship; the question though is will they be around when you need them or will they only be around when they need you?

Keep some friends at arms-length. There are few things more dangerous than a Fake Friend.

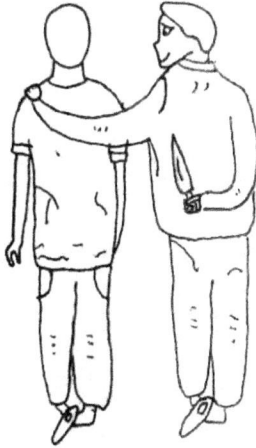

If life is a game and you want to win, you need good teammates (friends). In order to have good friends around you, you must be one yourself. This follows the Law of Attraction. You will attract what you are. Therefore, think of the qualities you would like to be surrounded by. Start by trying to always do the right thing, even if it is hard.

Good decisions are sometimes hard to make. Trust me though, making the wrong decision because it is easier now always ends up hurting worse later.

Clap when your friends win. Whether it is a competition they won or played well in, a goal they achieved, or a good deed they did, support them… and mean it. In return, you should see that same level of support when you win. If that support is not returned, you may want to reconsider who you are calling a *friend*. Stop hanging around those who do not want you to win. Find those that clap for you when you win and keep them close. Find those that do not and cut them loose.

Show people they can trust you. Without trust, there is nothing. If they confide in you to keep something private, you must. Show them that you are trustworthy… that is a quality that is so hard to find these days.

Your friends and family members can either be anchors or sails to the ship of your life's journey. Sails will help you level up and get to the next port of growth and achievement… anchors will not.

What you tolerate from those around you will show up more frequently (i.e. being taken advantage of, negativity, gossip, being abused, etc.). Quit tolerating the bad behaviors from those you are surrounded by; this includes friends and family.

Change your mind or change the scenery around you. Meaning… quit tolerating the behavior and instead, let them know it bothers you. If they choose not to change their behavior when they are around you, then change your scenery… Leave.

Be careful being so available to certain friends. There are some friends that will take advantage and take you for granted; they will take for granted your time, your support, and your love. I am sure you have heard of the idea that some people mistake your *kindness* for *weakness.* This can happen by sometimes being so available or always putting others' needs ahead of yours. While it is important to be considerate of others, never forget to take care of your needs and well-being also. It is all about balance.

Your goals, dreams, and visions are not for everyone to understand. In fact, there will be some people (including friends and family members) that will put down your dreams, possibly even laugh in your face about them. Again, quit expecting everyone to accept or understand your goals and dreams. In fact, if you find that there is not anyone who is ridiculing your ideas and vision, maybe you are not dreaming big enough. Your Goals should even make you sweat! If they do not, maybe they are too small.

People tend to morph into what they are surrounded by, so consider this:

Successful people tend to hang around successful people. Lazy people tend to hang around lazy people.

Bad people tend to hang around bad people, and convicts tend to hang around other convicts.

Leadership

Help Them, Help You

Leaders sometimes have to walk alone. Leaders are the first to be blamed but the last to receive credit. Leaders have much more responsibility than others; your concern is not just your ability and performance, but the abilities and performances of those you lead. It can definitely be a lonely journey, and is not for the weak. However, only so many in the world can ever be so lucky to call themselves a leader. You were chosen to be a leader because others saw leadership qualities in you. You displayed a certain level of understanding of your craft, that others **trust** you to lead them, their team or their loved ones. So obviously, you are doing something right. Average people are not asked to lead, overachievers are.

A true leader is measured by how many people they help achieve their goals (in order to get what you want you must first help others get what they want).

Most people wait for failure to occur before correcting or improving themselves. I always use the example of Tiger Woods at the height of his competitive career. It seemed like it was every week that he was tinkering or changing his golf swing; this was while he was ranked #1 in the world! He still felt there was something he could be doing better. This was definitely a driving force for winning as much as he did. He never allowed himself to get comfortable or become complacent in his abilities.

"Great leaders try to improve even when they succeed." – Tom Brady

Why wait? Why not continually improve and grow so failure does not happen? When many people win in the sports arena or in the game of life, they quit improving. They believe that if they continually do the same thing over and over, their results will stay the same. However, what they forget to consider is that their competition *is* continually changing things. **Your competition is not content with their results if YOU are winning.** This is why you must also continue to improve.

One way to improve your results is to help others around you (especially those on your team), improve. Michael Jordan found that if he helped his team improve, he would get what he wants in the end... a championship – or six!

Great leaders show their abilities more through their actions and less with their words. Being a great leader makes those around them better. When those around you get better, **YOU GET BETTER!**

Imagine you have a championship game coming up soon. The people you surround yourself with are your team members. What can you do to lift them up and have them perform to their best abilities then, in turn, bring home the championship? That championship could be an actual ring or trophy, or it may be the successes and wins in the Game of Life.

By leading those to get where they are going, you yourself will become more clear on your goals and direction.

"You can have everything in life you want, if you just help other people get what they want."
– Zig Ziglar

By being a great leader, you also sharpen your skills. By being able to explain skills and techniques to others, it helps you to solidify those skills and techniques in your own mind.

A leader helps those to feel certain when they are in an uncertain place.

An open mind always creates and brings new opportunities. Instead of thinking, "This will not work," or "This is not for me," ask yourself, "How can this work for me?"

When you are the leader, you have less direction given by others. This means you have to be willing to learn and figure out things by yourself. That is why it is important to always keep that "student" mentality... always be a student and continually learning ways and methods to improve. While leaders at times have less accountability, they have more responsibility. They are now responsible for others and their well-being. It is no longer about you, it is about them, your team. That team may be an actual sports team, the staff at your workplace, or your family. KNOW YOUR TEAM. Some members of your team are motivated and respond differently than others.

"Some are motivated by the carrot, and some are motivated by the stick." – Tom Brady

All great leaders have great visions. People love to be around those that have great vision. As a leader, you have to "sell" others on your vision. Do not take the word "sell" wrong. Selling a vision means that person believes so deeply in a goal or dream that it becomes contagious. The best way to "sell" a dream or vision is by living it yourself and by doing it yourself. Great leaders lead by example.

That vision could be a championship, a goal, a house, a movement – whatever!

Hustle

Develop Your Hustle Muscle

During your hustle (your journey to success), remember to take a day or two to do <u>nothing</u>! This is your time to recharge, reflect, relax, and rebuild that desire to hustle again!

To reiterate from earlier, there will be downturns and unexpected obstacles that will appear on your journey. Remember that journey to your Goal is not a straight line. There will be plateaus and valleys. However, you have two ways to treat every downturn or setback (this includes friendships, business, economy, relationships, etc.). It can either be a tragedy or an opportunity. The masses treat every setback or obstacle as a tragedy. It is all negative and destroys the rest of their day, week, or even month! Champions treat these obstacles as an opportunity to learn and grow. When a setback occurs, be thankful you are learning how to handle these situations early in your journey. It all depends on how *you* choose to view these challenges. It can either be a negative or a positive. Is it an opportunity for change and growth or is it a tragedy that gives you an excuse to quit, giving you another reason to take the easy or average route. Quit relying on your government, political party, race, gender, or skin color to get you places. Remember, the only free cheese is in a mousetrap. Quit blaming those same factors as to why you are in your current situation. Blame and excuses do not help you or your situation.

Come from the school of thought that your hustle determines your salary. The harder you work, the luckier you get. No one wants to team up with someone who owns the victim role. People definitely do not want another individual to take care of. However, when people recognize your hustle, you begin to draw attention and that is when opportunities begin to present themselves.

D's were not celebrated in school, but they take you far outside of school. D's are good grades in the school of hustle. Discipline, Determination, and Drive… with those 3 D's, anything is achievable. Whatever it is you want to achieve, do not stop until you make yourself proud. The best way to get started is to stop dreaming, and start doing. Stop trying to make sure everything is perfect before you start – just start! If you are Disciplined, Determined, and Driven, you will figure out the rest as you go, I promise. If it is easy, it is probably not worth it.

"If it is meant to be, it is up to me."
– Dan Nielsen

God does have a plan for you. His plan, though, is not to wake you up, make your meals, pay your rent, get you to work, and carry your lazy ass to the finish line. His plan is more of a partnership and less of an entitlement. How you live today totally dictates how you will live tomorrow.

Look at what the greats are doing, and use that path to get your start. Then find out what they are not doing, and do that to separate yourself from the pack and everyone else. Again, find your "It", your X-Factor; that thing that makes you different from everyone else. If you want to develop an above average attitude, start treating each day, week, and years of your life as quarters in a game. Just because you lose one quarter or the half does not mean the game is lost. For example, just because you have a bad morning does not mean the day is lost. Divide your day, week, or month into quarters… just like a game.

On Achieving Goals

Where focus goes, energy flows. Focus is the human superpower.

1. Focus on what you want; be clear.

2. Take massive action.

3. Be grateful.

"Being Grateful Brings Greatness." – Sean Ramey

You do not get what you want, you get what you work for.

Quit giving yourself away for free; if people do not pay, they do not pay attention and they do not pay respect.

Do not expect others to see your vision as clearly as you do. Remember that if your Goals do not draw some hate and even make you sweat, they are probably too small.

True success is being able to live how you want and say what you want in order to help others succeed. This is where you become a great leader. In order to achieve what you want, help others achieve what they want.

Obsession can be a powerful tool when you focus, and focus on the right things. There has been a negative stigma attached to the word obsession. Obsession is just a tool that can be used for good or bad; it depends on the user.

Do what everyone else is doing and you will end up doing the same as they did. Again, it is great to see what others have done to get started, but what is going to make you different? If there is nothing that makes you different or makes you stand out, you end up getting lost at the bottom. It is always crowded at the bottom. If you always take the same path, you will always get the same average results.

Extraordinary people do the extra things ordinary people do not do. So, look at what others in your field are doing, and do what they are not doing!

Success should never be an option. Success is your job; it is your duty. When you start believing it, you begin achieving it. Trust me, there are so many more successful people who are dumber than you and I. I have met dozens. Yet, they found something they were not willing to give up on. They stayed focused on their goal, and stayed driven and committed until they reached it.

There needs to be continual growth; spiritually, emotionally, physically, and mentally.

Raising our standards ALWAYS ensures our growth in life. A new grade level in school, a new job or trade, a new town, a new activity. Continue to raise those standards and you will continue to see growth.

What got you where you currently are probably will not get you to where you want to be. In order to achieve higher levels, there needs to be better methods, otherwise you would currently be where you want to be. If you are where you strived to be, GREAT! Congratulations! Just do not get too comfortable as a competitor, business owner, parent, spouse, etc. Complacency is a silent killer. It is perfectly fine and even healthy to be grateful for where you are currently at, but let's broaden those horizons and AIM higher. You *are* capable of so much more than what you give yourself credit for.

Final Thoughts

Imagine yourself as a boat. The water around you is life. Your thoughts and attitude are your map and navigation system. Your skills are your motor. The people you surround yourself with are either anchors or sails. When your navigation or motor fails (and sometimes they will), it will be those who you surround yourself with that will either keep you moving or keep you anchored in one spot on your way to the "Port of Success".

Remember that you will attract what you are. Before anyone will like you, you must first like yourself. How can you expect anyone to love you if you do not first love yourself? It is amazing how many continually search for others to make them happy. You will not find others to make you happy until **you** can make yourself happy, FIRST! You will always attract what you are.

You will never see a negative person who is grateful. Sadly, you cannot achieve **Greatness** without being **Grateful**. It is impossible to stay angry when you have gratitude. So, if you change your attitude, you will end up changing the scenery around you. Gratitude is the base for prosperity and success. Be grateful for where you are at and be grateful for the journey you are on. There are countless people who would give everything they have to be where you currently are.

The greater things in life can only be accessed by the stairs... the elevator is out of order. It will always be out of order! There is no elevator that leads you to success. The stairs you take will give you the skills you need in order to achieve the level of Greatness you are searching for.

On another note, quit saying Time is Money. Time is **_not_** money. Time is more valuable. You can make more money, but you cannot make more time. You can waste your money, and get it back. You cannot waste time. When you waste it, it is gone forever.

If your happiness is dependent upon how you think people should act… they will leave you being a very unhappy person. People will continue to disappoint you. It is how you react to that disappointment that matters. Did you learn from it? Do you know how to handle it when it happens again? Or, do you plan on wishing or hoping it does not happen again? Let me save you the suspense; it WILL happen again. Learn how to deal with it. How you react to these situations is all that matters!

"Expectations traded for appreciation changes your state instantly." – Tony Robbins

Instead of allowing life to happen to you (reactive), attack life and make things happen (proactive). You can either let things happen <u>to</u> you or you can let things happen <u>for</u> you. This is the victim vs. victor mindset. When you begin to see things happening *for* you, you become the victor.

The only thing certain is change. You will always be stressed if you always search for certainty. If you are searching for change but struggle achieving it, remember that change is never a matter of ability. It is always a matter of motivation. How bad do you wish things were different? If you are not able to change, your situation must not be bad enough for you *to* change.

In life, you do not get what you want, you get what you work for. You get what you obsess over and focus on, and the more you **give**, the more you **get**.

Information or knowledge is nothing without ACTION. Knowledge is your vehicle, and action is your fuel. Without action, all that knowledge is useless. I have been to countless seminars and conventions, and I always wonder how many people will actually apply what they have learned when they get home. Most get excited, pumped up, and buy all the products, only to go back to what they were doing before the seminar or convention. Remember, there are Dreamers, and then there are Do-ers.

My faith, as a Christian, helped me through some tough times and continues to guide and push me to continually achieve. For you, whether it is Buddha, Brahman, Confucius, Allah, the Universe, whatever your higher power may be, use it and fight for it. It seems that all those who have achieved Greatness fight for something greater than themselves.

Some believe Champions or the Greats never have fear. This is incorrect. They just have an ounce more courage. Their courage allows them to take action even though they are afraid.

You have to remember that you do not get what you think you deserve in life. You get what you work for. You get what you plan for. You get what you focus on. And in the end, the world gives you what you deserve.

Improving your life over time only happens when you improve your standards and expectations.

The decisions and actions we make today will determine the life we will have tomorrow. With that, Life is a circle. There **will** be good times and there **will** be bad times. Enjoy it when times are good – and when times get bad, know it is just temporary.

The older we get, the more we search for what is "comfortable". I believe that is when aging accelerates. Get busy living or get busy dying. There are only two things that happen to you every day; you are either Growing or you are Dying, you can only choose one.

Quit allowing the past to jail your future. Many allow their past to hold them back from what they can achieve in the future. No one is arguing that your past was not hard. No one is saying that you didn't experience horrible trauma. Are you going to allow that night, that week, those years, to imprison you from the joys of your future? Quit being a slave to your past. You are the Master of your future, not a slave to your past. Stop letting those experiences destroy your future. If you do, those past experiences have won.

Favorite Quotes

I love quotes. They are short, to the point, and make an impact. They spur your thoughts and emotions. Here are a few of my favs. Enjoy!

"The only thing necessary for the triumph of evil is for good men to do nothing." – Edmund Burke

"Argue for your limitations and sure enough, they are yours." – Richard Bach

"If you risk nothing, then you risk everything." – Geena Davis

"You can do anything, but not everything."
– David Allen

"People may doubt what you say, but they will believe what you do." – Lewis Cass

"Why ask, 'Why me?' Instead ask, 'Why not me?'"
– Mike Tyson

"One does not discover new lands without consenting to lose sight of the shore for a very long time." – André Gide

"It's not that someone hasn't found themselves yet, it's that they haven't created themselves yet. They themselves are makers of themselves."
– James Allen

"Your focus on hating yesterday is killing your opportunity to love tomorrow."
– Gary Vaynerchuk

"Being grateful brings greatness." – Sean Ramey

"Your past does not equal the future unless you live there." – Tony Robbins

"Your goals must always be greater than the obstacles you face." – Jesse Itzler

"How you do anything is how you do everything."
– Martha Beck

"I didn't come this far to only come this far."
– Tom Brady

"Tough times never last, but tough people do."
– Robert H. Schull

"...the more dishonest you become comfortable with in the name of making money, the more likely you are to get tripped up on your own bullshit." – Robert Irvine, Restaurant Impossible

"Whether you think you can or think you can't, you're right." – Henry Ford

"God punishes you by giving you everything you want." – Mike Tyson

"Attitude determines Altitude." – Anonymous

"Be nice to people on your way up because you will meet them on your way down."
– Wilson Mizner

"Do not share your big dreams with little people."
– Grant Cardone

"Your quality of life is where you live emotionally." – Tony Robbins

"Rip up the playbook; do life differently."
– Jesse Itzler

"A great attitude will not guarantee your success, but a bad one will guarantee your failure."
– Anonymous

"It is more important to have the mindset of a champion as opposed to the skillset of one."
– Mike Tyson

"Change your thoughts and you will change your world." – Norman Vincente Peale

"If they ever put me on the field, they will never take me off." – Tom Brady

"Don't fight or resist fear; align and go with it. Fear always exhausts first." – Tony Robbins

"As a man thinks, so does he become."
– Proverbs 23:7

"Some of you have big league dreams and backyard work ethic... and your parents applaud you for it." – Dawn Staley, Head coach of the South Carolina Women's Basketball team

"Your town does not owe you recreational facilities and your parents do not owe you fun. The world does not owe you a living. Develop a backbone, not a wishbone. You are important and you are needed." – John Tapene, Northland College principal

"The only thing constant is change." – Heraclitus

"Make those choices now so you are not making excuses later." – Sean Ramey

"I need new haters. The old ones became my fans." – Zlatan Ibrahimović

"You can have success or you can have excuses. You cannot have both." – Grant Cardone

"You will accomplish more through movement than you ever will through meditation."
– Gary Halbert

"If you spend too much time working on your weaknesses, all you end up with is a lot of strong weaknesses." – Dan Sullivan

"Those who have their health have 1,000 dreams; those who do not have health have only one."
— Chinese Proverb

"New levels create new devils." — T.D. Jakes

"The greater the setback, the greater the comeback." — Tim Storey

"Good is the enemy of Great." — Tony Robbins

"Confidence brings success, success brings confidence." — Mike Tyson

"The world doesn't care about your excuses."
— Sean Ramey

"Genius is one percent inspiration and ninety-nine percent perspiration." – *Thomas Edison*

"The dream is free, but the hustle is sold separately." – *Rick Ross*

"Worry does not take away tomorrow's troubles; it takes away today's peace." – *Ed Mylett*

"One day, the people that didn't believe in you will tell everyone how they met you."
– *Johnny Depp*

"Most men die at age twenty-five, but we just don't get around to burying them until they are seventy-five." – *Benjamin Franklin*

"Time is the only thing that is equal for all humans. Don't ever say you don't have enough of it." – Tony Robbins

"The truth will set you free, but it will make you miserable at first." – Mike Tyson

"Quit worrying about things out of your control, focus only on what you can." – Tom Brady

"Separate emotion from action. How you feel has zero to do with how you perform."
– Grant Cardone

"My confidence comes from my experience, not from my lies." – Sean Ramey

"Are you hurt or are you injured?" – *Rick Ross*

"Your past and your present do not equal your future." – *Ed Mylett*

"I'm cocky in prediction, I am confident in preparation, but I am always humble in victory or defeat." – *Conor McGregor*

"You are your own worst enemy. You waste precious time dreaming of the future instead of engaging in the present." – *Robert Greene*

"Obsession is a tool; it's neither good nor bad. You can use it to destroy or to build, just like any other tool." – *Grant Cardone (reworded)*

"When I let go of what I am, I become what I might be." – Lao Tzu

"I will be the master of my future, and not a slave to my past." – Sean Ramey

Bonus Section:

On Raising Champions

Once a child recognizes the importance of work ethic, respect, and discipline, and then adopts them into their life, the world is theirs.

These are among the many qualities that are hard to find in today's current conditions. We could write several books as to why, but we are better off teaching the importance of them to our current and future generations. When things are given to you, you appreciate them for a day. When you work your ass off for something, you appreciate it forever.

We all agree that, as parents, we want to give our children some of the things that we never got or had the pleasure of experiencing. However, when everything is *given* and not *earned,* they are less appreciated and less meaningful.

By teaching them work ethic, we know they will be able to provide for themselves when their parents are long gone. By teaching them the importance of respect, we know they will be able to get along well with others, whether that is in a sports or work environment. By being respectful, they will gain admiration and trust, as well as be an example for others to follow. By teaching them the meaning and importance of discipline, they will be able to control their actions and thoughts in particular situations. They will also be able to focus on a task, even when the conditions become tough, by following a set of rules or regulations set by themselves or others.

You must show your kids the way or path. Children tend to learn best by example. Therefore, set an example that you would want them to follow. You will have to give them a push every once in a while on that path, but you must <u>never</u> carry them down that path. Allow them to fail, fall, pick themselves up, and figure things out themselves.

Somewhere along the line we confused giving our children a good life with making things easy for them. Remember, easy times make weak people. It is all about balance.

It is natural to give our children the things and experiences we did not have, but is it the right thing to give them everything?

The Path to Success for Our Youth:

Sports and competition for youth is vital to their wellbeing. Let them feel what winning is like and, for the love of God, let them feel what losing is like.

In life, you do not get what you want. You get what you obsess over. You get what you work for. You get what you focus on.

Quit having them believe they have to have their life all figured out by high school graduation. Let them

Live, Learn, and Laugh; and teach them to not do anything stupid that could affect their credit, their finances, or their health. That way when they finally figure things out, they are mentally, emotionally, physically, and financially ready to conquer life.

If you want your child to stand out and be different, teach them courtesy, respect, and work ethic. These are qualities that are rarely seen today, especially from our youth. Once they master these qualities, the world will be theirs for the taking. Courtesy is the New Cool.

Here is another way to have your child stand out: Teach them to always say "please" and "thank you," or to hold the door open for someone; this may lead to the door of opportunity being held open for them, one day. It is amazing how far a little courtesy can go!

Quit letting your child win at everything. This is crippling them for the future. They will not win at everything when they get older either, so let them begin to learn how to handle losses early.

It seems that every generation gets softer as time goes on. It was not too long ago that people complained about "helicopter parents". These were parents that hovered over every little thing their child did or got into. However, during the writing of this book, we now have "bulldozer parents". Those are parents that bulldoze every little bit of struggle, challenge, or hardship out of little Johnny or Sarah's way, only to cripple them as they get older because they do not know how to handle failure, loss, or challenges. So, Mom, Dad... do not be a bulldozer! Quit bubble-wrapping your kids because it makes them fragile!

If you want to put a unique or different picture of your child on social media that will stand out and grab attention, post a picture of them losing or shaking hands with the winner. We all know people tend to only post their wins. Rarely do parents brag about the fact that their kids (or themselves) just lost. Yet, what a way to stand out; showing that their kid not only knows how to win, but also knows how to handle defeat. Try posting #NoParticipationTrophies. It is hard to find younger competitors that know how to congratulate the winners. Sportsmanship is a fading quality that certainly needs to make a comeback. It is a vital life skill that will benefit them the rest of their lives.

Tough times make strong people. Easy times make weak people. Let them face adversity, and let them face it often and early.

Children can either work hard now (while they are young) and be happy later, or they can be happy now (slack off) and work hard forever.

By wanting your child to not cry small tears when they are small, you are ensuring that they will cry big tears when they are big.

Give your child more Vitamin "N". We could all use a bit more Vitamin N in our lives. The N I'm referring to is the word No.

No, they do not need every new version of iPad or iPhone. No, they do not need to hang with their friends every day after school. No, they do not need their bed made or room cleaned by you every day. No, they do not need a new toy or piece of candy every time you fill up your gas tank.

Just because they **want** does not mean they **need.** Get them used to hearing the word "No"; they will hear it a lot when they get older.

Teach them how to defend and stand up for themselves. If you do not know how, send them to someone who can teach them. Teach them not to rely on others to protect themselves. Every human being should know the basics of self-defense and self-protection.

Teach them to speak up for themselves. One day in the near future, you will not be by their side and they will have to speak up and hopefully make the responsible choice.

When they learn how to defend and speak up for themselves, you will see a huge improvement in their confidence, self-esteem, and respect.

When at a restaurant, let them order for themselves. Teach them the words "please" and "thank you". This helps them with confidence and speaking up, and gets them comfortable with social interactions and respecting others.

If they are purchasing something, have them walk up to the counter to pay and get their change. This teaches them the buying and selling process, and they can begin to understand the value of a dollar. The sooner your child learns the value of a dollar, the better. Let them see how quickly it spends and goes.

Even more importantly, show them how fast it grows when they save and invest it.

Teach them that life is all about **_Balance_**; to play hard, you must first work hard. There will be happy times and there will be sad times. They need to be grateful when times are good because it is temporary, and they need to keep their heads up when times are bad because it is also temporary. Too much of anything can be bad. It is important for them to know there must be rainy days, in addition to sunny days. There will be happy times and there will be sad times. When there are hard times, there will also be easy times.

If you have never let your child fall, how will they ever learn to pick themselves up? By letting them fail or lose, a vital lesson occurs. This teaches them that if things do not go their way, they must find another way. They must try again, adapt, and improve until things work out the way they planned.

Let your kids know that while you may not always say the right thing or do the right thing, you are <u>trying</u> for the <u>right</u> outcome.

You, just like your parents, are trying to figure out the journey of life and are trying to do the best you can with what you have. Life did not come with an instruction manual, but when we listen and observe, we are able to avoid making the mistakes that others before us have made.

I never worry about kids that have good work ethic, discipline, and respect. They will go far in whatever they choose because almost no one (especially their age) possesses those qualities.

We all need some practice (including our children), in facing adversity. Life, in many ways, has made things so much easier for us. Whether it is the remote control, the iPhone, or the internet, we all have gotten quite lazy. So, when adversity shows its face, be thankful that it has. What great training for the future in handling obstacles and challenges. Every time they face adversity, they get better at handling it. This is not to say that I believe children's lives are 100% easy; however, many aspects are, such as air conditioning, phones, remotes, internet, their own bedroom's t.v., and iPads, to name a few. If you are in the camp that believes children's lives are tougher today than previous generations, then you must agree that they need practice facing adversity, loss, failure, etc. If you are in the camp that believes kids are coddled, soft, and have everything handed to them too easily, then *I know* you think they need practice in facing adversity, loss, failure, etc.

Notes

About the Author

Sean Ramey was born in Louisville, Kentucky to John and Jaynee Ramey. His parents enrolled him in Martial Arts at a young age due to his shyness. He is now a 7th Degree Black Belt, and has owned and operated one of the region's largest martial arts schools for the last 26 years. His students have gone on to attend institutions such as Yale, Harvard, and Westpoint. Many have won numerous titles on the State, Collegiate, National, and International levels. Above all, countless have become upstanding citizens, loving parents, supportive spouses and siblings, straight A students, CEOs, and servicemen and servicewomen.

Sean has starred in several network television shows and performed in numerous feature films. Sean continues to speak, act, and teach martial arts to this very day.

Enjoy what you read? I would love to hear from you! Connect with me on Instagram: @TheSeanRamey or email me at ChampsInLife1@gmail.com.

www.ChampsInLife.com

www.ingramcontent.com/pod-product-compliance
Lightning Source LLC
Chambersburg PA
CBHW060335050426
42449CB00011B/2758